Even More HYMN CREATIONS

10 UNIQUE PIANO SOLO ARRANGEMENTS
by Randall Hartsell

ISBN 978-1-5400-7250-4

WILLIS MUSIC

EXCLUSIVELY DISTRIBUTED BY

HAL•LEONARD®

Visit Hal Leonard Online at
www.halleonard.com

Contact us:
Hal Leonard
7777 West Bluemound Road
Milwaukee, WI 53213
Email: info@halleonard.com

In Europe, contact:
Hal Leonard Europe Limited
42 Wigmore Street
Marylebone, London, W1U 2RN
Email: info@halleonardeurope.com

In Australia, contact:
Hal Leonard Australia Pty. Ltd.
4 Lentara Court
Cheltenham, Victoria, 3192 Australia
Email: info@halleonard.com.au

PREFACE

As I complete this third collection of hymn creations, time marches on. I recently retired as director of music for a wonderful congregation after 28 years of service. This collection contains many hymn arrangements that I used during my last year at the church.

My congregation was always open to new music and ideas. They especially enjoyed a fresh look and sound of a familiar hymn tune. The creative use of modern harmonies can wake up our ears to the rich, contemporary sounds of our ever evolving church music heritage. I always enjoy the congregation's excitement on hearing an old favorite tune in a new, fresh way.

Feel free to release your own creative ideas as you perform these arrangements. Fill your performance time with energy, joy, and freedom as you create an expressive interpretation of this music.

May you enjoy the spiritual bond you develop with your congregations as you share the pieces in *Even More Hymn Creations*.

Randall Hartsell

CONTENTS

Amazing Grace

Words by John Newton
Traditional American Melody
Arranged by Randall Hartsell

Moderately, with energy

For the Beauty of the Earth

Words by Folliot S. Pierpoint
Music by Conrad Kocher
Arranged by Randall Hartsell

8

Great Is Thy Faithfulness

Words by Thomas O. Chisholm
Music by William M. Runyan
Arranged by Randall Hartsell

Moderately and freely

Let Us Break Bread Together

Traditional Spiritual
Arranged by Randall Hartsell

Love Divine, All Loves Excelling

Words by Charles Wesley
Music by John Zundel
Arranged by Randall Hartsell

A Mighty Fortress Is Our God

Based on the hymn by Martin Luther
Arranged by Randall Hartsell

With pedal, create a blur

Clear pedal

There Is a Balm in Gilead

African-American Spiritual
Arranged by Randall Hartsell

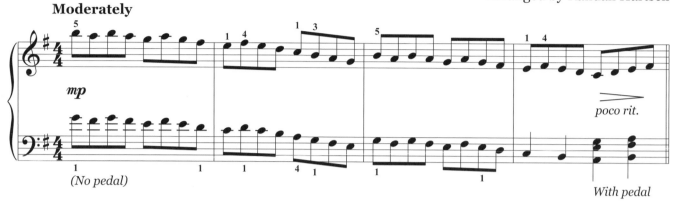

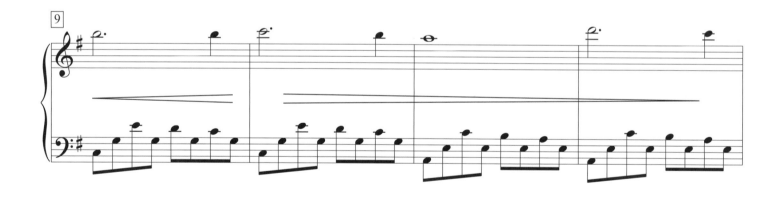

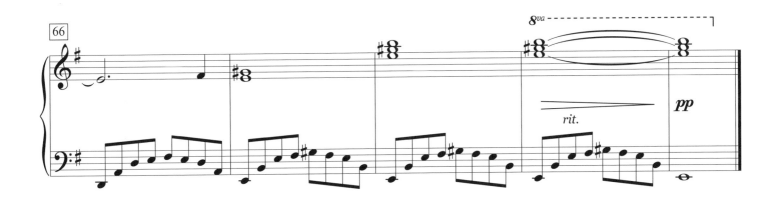

We Gather Together

Netherlands Folk Hymn
Music from *Nederlandtsch Gedenckclanck*
Arranged by Randall Hartsell

Were You There?

Traditional Spiritual
Arranged by Randall Hartsell

Andante e cantabile

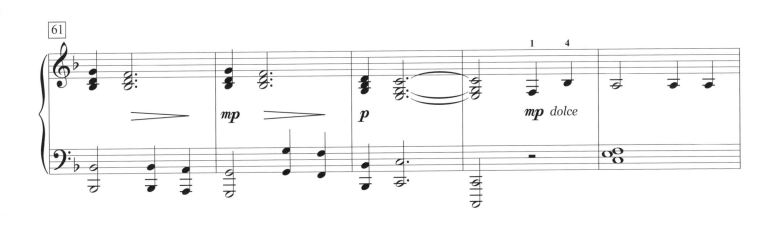

This Little Light of Mine

Traditional
Arranged by Randall Hartsell

MORE PIANO SOLO ARRANGEMENTS
by Randall Hartsell

Hymn Creations

HL00416925

Amazing Grace • The Ash Grove
• Be Thou My Vision • Beach Spring (Lord,
Whose Love In Humble Service) • Come,
Thou Fount of Every Blessing • Fairest Lord
Jesus • Holy, Holy, Holy • Kingsfold (My Soul
Proclaims Your Greatness) • Now Thank We All
Our God • When Morning Gilds the Skies.

More Hymn Creations

HL00122464

All Things Bright and Beautiful • Blessed
Assurance • Break Thou the Bread of Life
• Come, Thou Almighty King • Glorious
Things of Thee Are Spoken • He Leadeth Me
• Immortal, Invisible • Jesus, the Very Thought
of Thee • My Hope Is Built on Nothing Less
• 'Tis So Sweet to Trust in Jesus.

Christmas Creations

HL00416823

Angels We Have Heard on High • Away in a Manger • Carol of the Bells • Deck the Hall • God Rest Ye Merry, Gentlemen • Good King Wenceslas • Jingle Bells • Joy to the World • O Come, Little Children • Silent Night • We Three Kings of Orient Are.

More Christmas Creations

HL00416916

Christmas Time Is Here • Do You Hear What I Hear • Here Comes Santa Claus (Right down Santa Claus Lane) • A Holly Jolly Christmas • I'll Be Home for Christmas • Let It Snow! Let It Snow! Let It Snow! • Rudolph the Red-Nosed Reindeer • Silver Bells • Wonderful Christmastime.

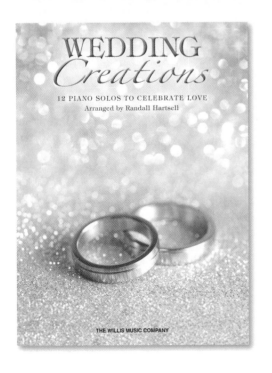

Wedding Creations

HL00113014

Air (Handel) • Allegro Maestoso (Handel) • Arioso (Bach) • The Heavens Declare (Marcello) • Jesu, Joy of Man's Desiring (Bach) • Love Divine, All Loves Excelling (Prichard) • Ode to Joy (Beethoven) • Rondeau (Mouret) • Trumpet Voluntary (Clarke). Plus 3 original pieces: Adagio from the Heart • Chanson d'amour • Unity of Love.

BIOGRAPHY

Randall Hartsell began his music career as a piano performance and pedagogy major at East Carolina University. His attention turned quickly to the joys of piano composition. Growing up in North Carolina provided inspiration to express the beauty of his native state with lyrical, romantic pieces. His music has expanded beyond the expressive melodic music to include advanced and technically demanding compositions as well as creative elementary pieces. As a past adjunct faculty member of Pfeiffer University and the University of North Carolina at Charlotte, Mr. Hartsell brings a wide range of experiences that enrich the lives of both students and teachers.

Mr. Hartsell has been a featured composer and contributor to Clavier Companion, and he is a frequent judge of local composition contests and the National Guild of Piano Teachers composition division.

His workshops help students and teachers foster creativity and interest in composition as well as develop essential technical skills and ease in improvisation. In addition, his experience as music director of a Lutheran church has enabled him to pen a variety of Christmas, hymn, and wedding collections.